# A HOUSE
# NOT
# DIVIDED

**DEFEATING THE
SPIRIT OF DIVISION**

KENNETH COPELAND

## *A House NOT Divided*
*Defeating the Spirit of Division*

ISBN 978-1-60463-280-4     30-0079

20 19 18 17 16 15            6 5 4 3 2 1

© 2015 Kenneth Copeland

Kenneth Copeland Publications
Fort Worth, TX 76192-0001

For more information about Kenneth Copeland
Ministries, visit kcm.org or call 1-800-600-7395
(U.S. only) or +1-817-852-6000.

# A HOUSE NOT DIVIDED

## DEFEATING THE SPIRIT OF DIVISION

I want to warn you about a destructive spirit working in the world today, and put you on high alert that this spirit of division has been assigned against *your* household and against *your* church. In fact, the spirit of division has been sent on assignment by the devil to harass your nation and hinder the entire Body of Christ.

Shocking as that may sound, it's the truth.

It's also nothing new. It's been going on for centuries, and the devil knows, far better than most believers, just how destructive a force division actually is.

Of course, he didn't figure that out on his own. Jesus taught about it in Mark 3:24-26. He said, "If a kingdom be divided against itself, that kingdom cannot stand. And if a house be divided against itself, that house cannot stand. And if Satan rise up against himself, and be divided, he cannot stand, but hath an end."

But read what else Jesus said in the next verse: "No man can enter into a strong man's house and spoil his goods, except he will first bind the strong man; and then he will spoil his house" (verse 27).

When we quote that verse, we usually think of Satan as the strongman. We think of binding him and spoiling his house—and that's true.

But, let me remind you of something: Satan is not the strongman any longer. He's been conquered! The Bible says Jesus defeated him and made a spectacle of him (Colossians 2:15). In the eyes of God, there *is* a strongman in the earth today, but it's not the devil. It's the Body of Christ.

Ephesians 6:10 declares: "Finally, my brethren, be strong in The LORD, and in the power of *his* might." We are the strongman. The household of God holds all authority and power in the earth—authority and power that came from Jesus Himself through His mighty conquest.

Because of that conquest, Satan can't enter your house unless he can first get you into bondage. He is a defeated foe. He has to bring the bondage to you and get you to enter into it. He doesn't have the authority to go around doing whatever he wants to do. He seeks "whom he *may* devour" (1 Peter 5:8), but he doesn't always find someone to devour.

Jesus told His disciples in Matthew 28:18-20, "All power is given unto me in heaven and in earth. Go ye therefore, and teach all nations, baptizing them in the name of the Father, and of the Son, and of the Holy Ghost: Teaching them to observe all things whatsoever I have commanded you: and, lo, I am with you always, even unto the end of the world."

Do you see that? He said, "All authority has been given to Me both in heaven and in earth. Therefore, *you* go into all the earth and take My Name, and in My Name *you* cast out the devil."

So, who has the power? We do! The real power is ours. It has been delegated to us and belongs to us.

# A Spirit of Deception

The only power the devil has against us is through deception—illusion. He lies to us and then waits for us to fall for those lies, because he can't do a single thing about plundering our house until he has us bound. But, make no mistake about it. Once he has us bound, he will spoil our goods until *we* do something about it.

When Jesus' disciples came to Him asking, "What shall be the sign of thy coming, and of the end of the world?" (Matthew 24:3), Jesus got straight to the point. He gave them a warning: "Take heed that no man deceive you. For many shall come in my name, saying, I am Christ; and shall deceive many" (verses 4-5).

Look at verse 6, and read what Jesus said was going to happen: "And ye shall hear of wars and rumours of wars: see that ye be not troubled."

We're living in the midst of those troubling times right now. Threats of war and acts of terrorism and aggression blanket the front pages of newspapers and magazines, and lead the top stories on the evening news. The reports are all over the media, and so is the fear they produce.

But what do wars and rumors of wars have to do with division?

Everything!

In Matthew 12:25 Jesus said, "Every kingdom divided against itself is brought to desolation; and every city or house divided against itself shall not stand." In Mark 3:25, He repeated those words: "And if a house be divided against itself, that house cannot stand."

I don't know about you, but that reads pretty clear to me. The house that's divided *will* fall. It's not a probability. It's not likelihood. It's inevitable. Once you begin operating in a spirit of division, your house becomes weak—and Jesus said *it will fall*.

I remember praying one day, repenting before God about something critical I'd said regarding another preacher. When I finished, God said to me, *It's a good thing you did that.* Suddenly, I realized how serious this thing was. God knew that if I divided myself from someone else in His Body, I would guarantee my own failure. I would fall.

That's a dangerous thing not to know. It's even more dangerous to know it and not pay attention to it.

# Deception Breeds Division

So why don't we know this? Because we've been deceived. Remember what Jesus said in Matthew 24:4? He said, "Take heed that no man deceive you."

The spirit of division has told us, "That person over there doesn't believe the way you do. You can't compromise your principles, so don't be part of him." So it piously calls itself "noncompromise" when, in fact, it's a spirit of judgment and segregation. It's a spirit that causes division.

In 1 Corinthians, the Apostle Paul says something startling to the believers at Corinth. He first acknowledges they've been gifted with every spiritual gift, and then says they've had revelation from God and are lacking in nothing. But then, he moves over into some things regarding their spiritual growth. Some inner warring had taken place among these people, and a spirit of division had stopped them from maturing spiritually. Paul talks about it in 1 Corinthians 3:1-3:

> And I, brethren, could not speak unto you as unto spiritual, but as unto carnal, even as unto babes in Christ. I have fed you with milk, and not with meat: for hitherto ye were not able to bear it, neither yet now are ye able. For ye are yet carnal: for whereas there is among you envying, and strife, and divisions...."

Envying, strife and divisions had kept these people in a natural or carnal state. It had so stunted their spiritual growth that they were unable to under-stand some of the things Paul wanted to teach them. It had halted Paul's ability to effectively minister to them. Their carnal minds could not comprehend those things because the things of God must be *spiritually* discerned (1 Corinthians 2:14). What's worse, they didn't even realize it. Their house had begun to crumble before they even knew there was a crack in the foundation.

In essence, Paul was saying to them: "I came to bring you many things, but you couldn't receive them because the spirit of division was among you, and you were acting like a bunch of babies! I couldn't do much because you people were divided. A spirit of division created a split."

But here's an interesting point: In another of Paul's letters, one he wrote to the church at Ephesus about spiritual growth, he says, "But speaking the truth in love, [we] may grow up into him in all things, which is the head, even Christ" (Ephesians 4:15).

Compare "speaking the truth in love" to "envyings, strife and divisions." They are complete opposites. You can't do both at the same time. According to this verse, as you speak the truth in love, you grow up, or mature, spiritually. You move away from a spirit of division and into a spirit of love and reconciliation. Envy, fussing and separating from one another takes you back to spiritual babyhood.

Let's read Matthew 24:4-6 again, this time in *The Amplified Bible:*

> Be careful that no one misleads you [deceiving you and leading you into error]. For many will come in (on the strength of) My

13

name [appropriating the name which belongs to Me], saying, I am the Christ (the Messiah), and they will lead many astray. And you will hear of wars and rumors of wars; see that you are not frightened or troubled, for this must take place, but the end is not yet.

Notice that phrase in verse 5: "lead many astray." Another way of saying that is: "They will cause division among you."

The work of the spirit of division is to divide and conquer—to cause you to be tossed to and fro with all kinds of doctrines and differences of opinion that can result in division. That's what it's sent to do, and it's been doing a pretty good job for a long, long time!

How does it do that? By *magnifying* differences.

In the Church, for example, there are differences in denominations. There are the Catholics and the Protestants, the Baptists and the Pentecostals, the Methodists and the Episcopalians, and so on. In our relationships, there are differences between male and female, and in the family, differences between brother and sister. And, in the business world, there are differences between management and labor. Then, there are differences in personal preferences: I ride a Honda, he rides a Harley.

But, we must understand that division is not the same as difference. God created things to be different. But Satan comes along and magnifies those differences with a spirit of discord and resentment. The Spirit of unity, which is the Holy Spirit,

15

magnifies those differences *in love* so they actually draw us together where we can learn from and share with one another, making us stronger.

When we walk together in the strength of unity, we become dangerous to the devil because we touch all bases instead of just one here and there. *Together,* we're a whole—complete, nothing missing! *Together,* we're a force the devil can't reckon with.

What all that means is simply this: If we're ever going to become truly powerful in the kingdom of God, and any great threat to the devil, we're going to have to grow up—together. It won't be enough for just a few of us to grow up on our own and say "too bad" about everyone else. It doesn't work that way. We're all part of each other. We're one Body—the Body of Christ!

# A Weapon of Destruction

One of the greatest and most destructive influences from the spirit of division we've had to deal with through the years is *racism*. The Bible doesn't look at racism or deal with it like the world does, or as most people are trained to view it. There's a lot more to racism than color or culture—or sheer bigotry and prejudice. The root of racism is the spirit of division. Anytime the devil can cause a spirit of division or magnify difference, racism is in operation.

The spirit of division always magnifies differences into a spirit of hate. Reconciliation, on the other hand, magnifies any differences into a spirit of love and cooperation.

For example, one person says, "This is what happened," and another person says, "No, that's not the way it was." Then, a third person comes along and says, "You're both wrong. I was there. I saw it, and *this* is really what happened." The truth is, they all saw the same thing, but interpreted it differently. Division produces a spirit of hate, with each one criticizing the other because of disagreement. But love and reconciliation help them all get together to discuss what each one saw, and come into agreement.

From this perspective, you can see how dangerously destructive a spirit of division can be. It's like a sickness or disease: If you don't watch out, it will creep in any way it can and take over. The devil knows the only way he can get anyone into bondage is to get them outside of love and focusing on differences.

But, *you* don't have to fall into that trap. If you'll follow love, the spirit of

division will *never* be able to deceive
you and spoil your house.

## A Lesson in Love

One of the most amazing stories
I've ever heard along these lines is
about a man named Johnny Johnson,
former United States Assistant Secre-
tary of the Navy (Manpower and
Reserve Affairs). If you've never read
his book, *Beyond Defeat,* you need to.
It's one of those books that should be
required reading for every born-again
child of God, along with the Bible!

Johnny tells about his dad, a very
tall, powerful man whose ancestry was
African Watusi. He was a man who
had learned that love is beyond defeat.

When Johnny was a little fellow
just starting school, the little white
boys treated him very unkindly. So

Johnny's dad said to him, "Now son, listen to me. Don't get mad at those little boys."

When Johnny started to argue, his dad interrupted him. "No, you mustn't get mad at those little guys, Johnny. They have a serious problem they can't help. Their white skin lets too much sunshine into their brains. During the middle of the day—about the time you all go out to recess—their brains overheat. They don't even know what they're doing. That's the reason you're smarter than they are. It's not because they don't have as many brains as you do. It's just that your black skin won't let your brain overheat."

So Johnny went back to school thinking his brain was cool and that was the reason he was so smart. He started thinking that way and his grades began to improve.

When someone got ugly with him on the playground, he'd pray, "Oh, LORD Jesus, help him. His brain is overheating. I can tell from the way he's acting, his brain is so hot today, it's awful!"

Johnny prayed earnestly for these poor, little white boys and their over-heated brains. He treated them with such kindness and pity that it wasn't long until they fell in love with him. They thought Johnny Johnson was the greatest thing that walked on two feet.

By the time Johnny was old enough to understand what his dad had done, he'd already realized the powerful principle his father had proven to him: that love is beyond defeat. He figured out that faith works by love; love never fails; God never fails; and His WORD never fails.

You have to believe those things in order to keep love functioning in your spirit, and the spirit of division out. Because of what his dad told him, Johnny Johnson put aside any feelings he may have had that could have led to division between him and his schoolmates, and replaced them with love. Instead of allowing the situation to cause a spirit of division to develop that could have eventually turned into hatred, he chose to love his schoolmates and pray for them.

The definition of the word *division* means "separation by difference of opinion or feeling; disagreement; dissension." It's what Jesus warned against in Matthew 24:4 when He said, "Take heed that no man deceive you." But look back at that chapter for a moment, and notice what else Jesus said in verse 7, just after He told His disciples to "be not troubled," or afraid. He said, "For nation shall rise against nation, and kingdom against kingdom: and there shall be famines, and pestilences, and earthquakes, in divers places."

The word *nation* is translated *ethnos,* or "ethnic groups." In other words, Jesus could just as easily have said, "For ethnic group shall rise against ethnic group and country against country: and there shall be famines…."

Stop and think about it for a moment: nation against nation, ethnic group against ethnic group. We're in the middle of all of that right now on a worldwide scale. It's out there in practically every arena, only we haven't always classified it as "racism," and we haven't recognized it as a spirit of division. The truth is, *it's the same spirit,* and it's from the same devil.

All the division we're seeing in the world today is far more serious than most people realize. As we've seen, the devil himself is causing the division because he *is* the spirit of division, and there are devils under his command that have been sent to do his divisionary work.

But here's the good news: Satan knows the tremendous spiritual power that's unleashed through our unity. He knows that a house divided against itself will fall, but if we, the Body of Christ, will come together in the unity of our faith, we'll stand! We will arrive at the full measure of the stature of Christ (Ephesians 4:13). So, to keep us from that goal, the spirit of division will try to operate and gain a foothold in our personal lives, our church lives, our social lives and our family lives to divide and conquer.

But if we'll stay in love, we can't be defeated by the spirit of division. It can't get through where there's love. When we walk in love and don't allow a spirit of division, we're not going to fall. The Bible says that in love there is no occasion of stumbling (1 John 2:10). No stumbling, no falling!

A number of years ago, I was preaching in a church in Fort Worth, Texas. As I stepped out of the pastor's study to walk into the auditorium, the front doors opened and in walked a group of what we referred to back then as "hippies." It was obvious they hadn't come anywhere close to soap and water in a long time!

Something inside me recoiled, and I thought, *Where in the world are those kids going to sit?* Suddenly, I heard The LORD speak to me so loudly that I felt the impact of it in every cell of my body.

He said, *Don't you criticize a man's dirty feet until you're ready to wash them!*

It hit me so hard, it nearly bent me over. It felt like someone had stuck a hot poker right in the middle of me, and it went all the way through. Those words burned into my inner man.

As those kids walked into the auditorium, I could hear the whispers of the people when they saw them. One woman said out loud what I had thought a few minutes earlier, "My God, where are they going to sit?" I realized, *She needs to hear what I just heard.* So I went to the platform, stopped the service and told them exactly what God had told me.

That one moment changed the life of that church. It did the same thing to them it had done to me: It burned inside them.

At the close of the service, when everyone got up to leave, one man called out, "Would everyone just hold it a minute?" He said, "I think we ought not to leave here until we take up an offering and buy these young people some groceries. They look hungry to me. And, as far as my house is concerned, if any of them wants a hot shower or a bed to sleep in, they've got it. If they can wear any of my clothes, they can have them."

Everyone else in the congregation started agreeing with the man and saying, "Yes, that's right. Me, too!" Men started digging in their pockets and coming up with grocery money. The group of kids started splitting up, each of them going home with someone in the church that day.

That evening they all came back to the church. As I was preaching, one of

27

the kids interrupted me. "I just can't wait any longer," he said. "I have to tell you that Jesus Christ is now my LORD!"

Later on, they told the pastor, "We really don't want to leave here. Could we stay?" They stayed. Eight of them eventually entered into full-time ministry. Satan made a play for me that day, but he lost. The instant I looked at those young people that morning, the spirit of division magnified every possible difference to bring in hate and separation. But then the Spirit of God spoke. When the Spirit of God speaks, you have a choice: You can keep on following the spirit of division, or you can turn around and kick him out.

When the spirit of division got kicked out of that church that morning, reconciliation came. Where the spirit of division brings separation, the Spirit of God brings reconciliation, agreement and one accord. One word from God brought food into those kids' hands, brought them deliverance from drugs and the world, and changed their lives forever.

The Bible says God has reconciled us to Himself and has given us the ministry of reconciliation—to go tell others that He's not holding their trespasses against them (2 Corinthians 5:19). He's already forgiven them. He did it before any of us asked Him to. All we have to do is make the decision to receive it, and we're heaven-bound.

It doesn't make any difference what kind of clothes we wear or the color of our skin. It makes no difference where we live or where we were born. It's the fact that we are *re*born that counts!

The devil is determined to keep us

apart, to keep us operating in a spirit of division because he knows that when we come together, our revelation of God will be far greater than any one of us individually (or any one group of us) could ever receive on our own. The Apostle Paul prayed in Ephesians 3:16-19 that God would "grant you, according to the riches of his glory, to be strengthened with might by his Spirit in the inner man... that ye, being rooted and grounded in love, may be able to comprehend *with all saints* what is the breadth, and length, and depth, and height; and to know the love of Christ, which passes knowledge, that ye might be filled with all the fullness of God." *"With all saints"* means all of us. When we get together, a new comprehension of God becomes available—one that's a lot bigger than the one we have now.

For more than 45 years, The LORD has instructed me to teach on only a few things. He's led me to teach people mostly about faith and standing on His promises in His WORD. He's never had me teach much on end times. He gave that assignment to others like my friend Hilton Sutton, who has gone on to be with The LORD. That was his part. When I would hear Hilton teach, I got a revelation of God in that area that I couldn't have gotten by myself.

That's just as true for individuals as it is for ministries. My mother, for instance, prayed with her dear black friend and prayer partner for years. Do you know one of the reasons why she loved to pray with that wonderful woman so much? It's because she knew things about prayer my mother needed to know. Those weren't the kinds of things someone could sit down and explain. My mother had to spend time in prayer with her to learn them.

In the realm of spiritual things, you know things I need to know, and I know things you need to know. Jesus said, "Where two or three are gathered together in my name, there am I in the midst of them" (Matthew 18:20). What we have to do, primarily, is come together in the spirit—in faith.

We're *already* one. Jesus took care of that on the cross. Now, the Bible says, it's time for us to come together in the unity of our faith because when that happens, the power produced is far greater than the sum of our parts (Ephesians 4:13). If a thousand of us come together, we are more powerful than just a thousand people who have faith.

The devil knows that and is afraid

of it. That's why centuries ago, he sent the spirit of division to keep us apart. But if we'll listen to the Spirit of God, we won't fall for that spirit of division. Instead, we'll start getting a greater revelation of this reality than we've ever had before. We'll start seeing it from all sides. We'll see the truth and the tremendous miracle power available when we are in agreement—in one accord—together, in Jesus' Name (Matthew 18:19; Acts 2, 4:24-31).

So, if you're ready for that kind of miracle power in your life, say this out loud, right now: "Spirit of division, I'm serving you notice in the Name of Jesus, that my house is off limits to you. I'll not be deceived by you anymore! And, from now on, I'm not moved or offended by the differences between me and others. I'm moved by the Spirit of God. My ministry is the ministry of reconciliation. I love people because God loves people—no matter who they are. Whether anyone else loves me or not is not my business. I'm going to love them because that's what God has told me to do. That's my job, and I'm going to do it His way!"

Now, get ready for a new day and new power! Remember, divided, we fall. But when we come together, we stand. And, all of heaven backs us up—rejoicing!

# Prayer for Salvation and Baptism in the Holy Spirit

*Heavenly Father, I come to You in the Name of Jesus. Your Word says, "Whosoever shall call on the name of the Lord shall be saved" (Acts 2:21). I am calling on You. I pray and ask Jesus to come into my heart and be Lord over my life according to Romans 10:9-10: "If thou shalt confess with thy mouth the Lord Jesus, and shalt believe in thine heart that God hath raised him from the dead, thou shalt be saved. For with the heart man believeth unto righteousness; and with the mouth confession is made unto salvation." I do that now. I confess that Jesus is Lord, and I believe in my heart that God raised Him from the dead.*

*I am now reborn! I am a Christian—a child of Almighty God! I am saved! You also said in Your Word, "If ye then, being evil, know how to give good gifts unto your children: HOW MUCH MORE shall your heavenly Father give the Holy Spirit to them that ask him?" (Luke 11:13). I'm also asking You to fill me with the Holy Spirit. Holy Spirit, rise up within me as I praise God. I fully expect to speak with other tongues as You give me the utterance*

*(Acts 2:4). In Jesus' Name. Amen!*

Begin to praise God for filling you with the Holy Spirit. Speak those words and syllables you receive—not in your own language, but the language given to you by the Holy Spirit. You have to use your own voice. God will not force you to speak. Don't be concerned with how it sounds. It is a heavenly language!

Continue with the blessing God has given you and pray in the spirit every day.

You are a born-again, Spirit-filled believer. You'll never be the same!

Find a good church that boldly preaches God's Word and obeys it. Become part of a church family who will love and care for you as you love and care for them.

We need to be connected to each other. It increases our strength in God. It's God's plan for us.

Make it a habit to watch the *Believer's Voice of Victory* television broadcast and become a doer of the Word, who is blessed in his doing (James 1:22-25).

# About the Author

Kenneth Copeland is co-founder and president of nneth Copeland Ministries in Fort Worth, Texas, I best-selling author of books that include *How to cipline Your Flesh* and *Honor—Walking in Honesty, uth and Integrity*.

Since 1967, Kenneth has been a minister of the gospel of rist and teacher of God's WORD. He is also the artist on urd-winning albums such as his Grammy-nominated *Only Redeemed, In His Presence, He Is Jehovah, Just a Closer Walk Big Band Gospel*. He also co-stars as the character Wichita m in the children's adventure videos *The Gunslinger, venant Rider* and the movie *The Treasure of Eagle untain*, and as Daniel Lyon in the *Commander Kellie and the erkids*$_{TM}$ videos *Armor of Light* and *Judgment: The Trial Commander Kellie*. Kenneth also co-stars as a Hispanic lfather in the 2009 movie *The Rally*.

With the help of offices and staff in the United States, nada, England, Australia, South Africa, Ukraine and gapore, Kenneth is fulfilling his vision to boldly each the uncompromised WORD of God from the top this world, to the bottom, and all the way around. His nistry reaches millions of people worldwide through ily and Sunday TV broadcasts, magazines, teaching dios and videos, conventions and campaigns, and the orld Wide Web.

## When the Lord first spoke to Kenneth and Gloria Copeland about starting the *Believer's Voice of Victory* magazine...

He said: *This is your seed. Give it to everyone who ever responds to your ministry, and don't ever allow anyone to pay for a subscription!*

For more than 45 years, it has been the joy of Kenneth Copeland Ministries to bring the good news to believers. Readers enjoy teaching from ministers who write from lives of living contact with God, and testimonies from believers experiencing victory through God's Word in their everyday lives.

Today, the *BVOV* magazine is mailed monthly, bringing encouragement and blessing to believers around the world. Many even use it as a ministry tool, passing it on to others who desire to know Jesus and grow in their faith!

### Request your FREE subscription to the *Believer's Voice of Victory* magazine today!

Go to **freevictory.com** to subscribe online, or call us at **1-800-600-7395** (U.S. only) or **+1-817-852-6000**.

## We're Here for You!®

Your growth in God's WORD and your victory in Jesus are at the very center of our hearts. In every way God has equipped us, we will help you deal with the issues facing you, so you can be the **victorious overcomer** He has planned for you to be.

The mission of Kenneth Copeland Ministries is about all of us growing and going together. Our prayer is that you will take full advantage of all The LORD has given us to share with you.

Wherever you are in the world, you can watch the *Believer's Voice of Victory* broadcast on television (check your local listings), on the Internet at kcm.org, or on our digital Roku channel.

Our website, **kcm.org,** gives you access to every resource we've developed for your victory. And, you can find contact information for our international offices in Africa, Asia, Australia, Canada, Europe, Ukraine and our headquarters in the United States.

Each office is staffed with devoted men and women, ready to serve and pray with you. You can contact the worldwide office nearest you for assistance, and you can call us for prayer at our U.S. number, +1-817-852-6000, 24 hours every day!

We encourage you to connect with us often and let us be part of your everyday walk of faith!

Jesus Is LORD!

*Kenneth & Gloria Copeland*

Kenneth and Gloria Copeland